The Language of Listening

is dedicated in gratitude

to the "most excellent spirits"

who have blessed my path

with light on the journey.

Thank you.

The Language of Listening

Image and Prose

Pamella Allen

First published in the United States in 2014 by Pamella Allen

www.pamellaallen.com

First published in paperback in 2014

ISBN: 978-1-312-58544-7

Printed and bound in the USA

The Language of Listening

Image and Prose by Pamella Allen

The Time Is Now

They speak they demand

They implore from just beyond and just before

It is time they say, it is time to put ink to parchment.

With the force of enforced torment they speak all in turn

Mouths unseen words unheard but tangibly, they implore.

Not with a plea but a demand it is time

Ink to parchment they confirm

The time is at hand.

The time is at hand old soul, no time to hide

Behind flesh circumstance joy or pride.

Foot in ass, knife at throat, guided by one's own hand.

It is time, the time is now my love

They demand.

If you were blessed with the language of listening

What knowledge would sing to your Soul?

Kindred

Art is my religion, my cathedral among the trees.

Kindred to the Willow as I pass beneath her swinging leaves

To her I say a greeting and she again greets me.

Do you remember me she asked, we met through the iris lens

You sat with him and them into the evenings deep,

You gazed up at me as the river bends.

Yes I remember you and I remember the breeze,

The moon, she was full I believe

It was to you I prayed in the moons full bloom

As the trade winds touched your leaves.

Art is my religion my cathedral among the trees.

I assign a gender to my beloved Willow I call the Willow she.

Perhaps it is the grace of her fingers, her branches

And her leaves as they sway in the breeze,

Like billowing hair in plaits, braids, or dreads perhaps.

...

Kindred to the Willow tree, the Willow she speaks to me

Do you remember me? She asked again.

We first met as your tiny hands reached up to touch my swaying leaves.

Yes I uttered I remember you, as I passed into your green hues

I remember as your swaying leaves reached down to touch me.

It was then that art became my religion my cathedral among the trees.

The scent of your green soothed my breath

The velvet of your leaves caressed me

Your sweet redemption a blessing sheltered beneath your sway.

My voice cried up to the heavens in the shade of a burning day

As the river stream beneath my feet carried all the pain away.

Art is my religion my cathedral among the trees

Kindred to the Willow, the Willow she speaks to me,

All is well, all is well, all is well and as it should be

Kindred to the Willow tree, Willow remember me.

No Talisman

As each one left they said

You need no talisman to survive

You need only clarity to thrive.

As each one left they told me

Empathy is not your enemy

Compassion no sign of poverty.

Beauty is beauty is beauty is beauty

It cannot be drawn upon a face

It can only be made manifest with grace.

2 Tiny Elephants

Into my dreams they came,

Two tiny brown elephants in amber shades.

Into this home they came, open to the natural world outside

The two tiny elephants amber and perfect they came inside.

I wonder why from the wilds they came to me as I dreamt.

Where is your tribe, where is your mother, your aunts, your father?

Perhaps it is me I surmised perhaps I am the tribe.

As they entered I sought to protect them

From my curious felines but they had nothing to fear

As the felines cleaned the tiny brown elephants,

Licked them to comfort and erase their fears.

Pleased to give them shelter, for their shelter is mine,

Honored that in me their new home and their tribe they did find.

But from where do you come sweet little brown elephants in such a tiny size

And are those tears that are falling from your innocent eyes?

The Mighty Elephant

The mighty elephant sways to the violins tone.

But of course my love, yes of course

Within such immense beauty a pure soul finds a home.

We attribute the mark of the savage to the mighty beast.

But the true brute the only real savage

Walks on two feet.

Tall Grass

A maiden voyage for the girl child but no not the first.

Across a bridge, over a gully to a field of dry earth

And onward through a stand of tall trees to where wild horses feed.

Foreboding perhaps of many journeys to come such as these.

A maiden voyage but no not the first.

Across a bridge, over a gully to a field of dry earth and onward through the trees,

Through a stand of trees to where wild horses feed.

No fear is felt by the girl child as she proceeds,

Encircled by wild horses as they feed.

Her tiny body weaves through flanks, legs and tails as they sway

As the little girl child proceeds alone on her way.

Wild horses whisper in greeting and query

Who is this little one so fearless and so sweet,

To where do you journey alone on such tiny feet?

What is it little one what is it that you seek,

As you venture across a bridge, over a gully on dry earth and through the trees

To where we wild horses feed.

As you venture on alone into tall grass

And into mystery.

After Oceans

Walking the waters in Bermuda's trilogy

Pushed by trade winds flow through the static pop of the Caribbean Sea

Under currents sway to the amphitheaters of Epidaurus

As Medea screams Euripides.

Senses of olfactory burn with the man stench of earth

After two weeks of days on waters journey seeking rebirth.

Living the inconsequence of one's own humanity

As ocean walls swell trading sky for sea.

Listening in awe to the rhythms hush

As oceans and rains do meet.

Spun into a solace of reverence as oceans and rains again greet

As oceans in rains return and return in its cycle to complete.

After oceans

Land moves and sways beneath such humble feet

Returning and returning to the solace of the sea in all its grace

In all its grace to touch again the oceans sweet face.

The One

While we continue to take we are taken

While we continue to learn we unlearn

While we do we are undone.

We the chosen ones who in our purpose feel entitled to take,

We are taken. We do and we are undone.

But there is something else, is it the one?

There is something else, it too comes to take.

A great equalizer perhaps well beyond our reach,

There is something else it comes to teach.

But there is something else, is it the one?

Shall it sit us down upon this earthly ground?

Shall it press us beneath its earthly weight?

While we learn we unlearn, while we are taken we take.

A great equalizer perhaps well beyond our reach

There is something else it comes to teach.

No gods to save us, no mind, no body politic

No science to emulate. Not one of us is safe

As the great equalizer watches and waits.

Do you watch as your infant king starves to death?

Love

Love does not look like a beat down

Does not punch you in your face,

Love doesn't come at the end of a fist

No my sweet darling love does not look like this.

Love does not look like a beat down for the husband, the child or the wife

Love does not come in your back at the end of a butcher's knife.

Love does not look like hate or rage, does not want to scratch you in the eye

Love is not dictated by anybody's pride or by anybody's lie.

Remember your children are watching, what they see they replicate.

Love has many faces, love does forgive because forgiveness has its grace.

Love does not steal from you, love wishes to give not to take

Love, it does not manipulate.

Love does not look like a beat down

Does not leave you with scars on your mind, your body and your face.

Love won't break your bones or blacken your eye

If you believe that love looks like this, just know sweet darling that is a lie.

...

Love does not look like a beat down

If this is what you know of love, my heart it bleeds for you

Love has patients love is kind, love listens, it is beautiful it is true.

Love does not look like a beat down

Won't put its fingers around your throat.

The life out of you, love will never choke

Love breathes life into your soul and sings light into your breast.

Love is all strength, its very own force that strokes but never strikes

Love won't make you run, cower and hide into a cold dark night.

Love does not look like a beat down

Love is the face of compassion, the smile of a mother, a father, a child.

Love leads you to sit down by still waters love is always by your side.

Love sits you down gently and washes your soul clean in the rivers tide.

Love is the light of god that shines in everybody's eyes

Love is the light of god that shines in everybody's eyes

Love is the light of god that shines in everybody's eyes.

Supernova

Strike gently for the fire is white hot

It will blind your fragile eyes.

Strike gently for the fire is white hot

It will burn your tender flesh.

Strike gently for the fire is white hot

My love strike gently.

The vision of a supernova is a romantic notion

Sexy stunning from a distance safe,

Light years away and way up in space.

Mother And Child

What were her thoughts about our pending time lost?

Who would this baby child be she must have thought.

What would she know, how would she remember me

Into the land of memory what would this child hold of me?

As the hours passed beyond the rush of preparations met

What words did she utter, something must have been said

As she ventured into the land of the dead.

The usual platitudes? I will always be with you

Remember that your mother holds a love that is true.

What heartbreak what strength belied in those warm brown eyes?

As the baby girl wailed, cried

And clutched her mother's breast upon which her life relied.

What heartbreak what strength belied in those warm brown eyes?

As she gazed out to horizons far into a future never to be realized.

The greatest sacrifice was both hers and mine.

The greatest sacrifice was our time

Farewell to the mother

Farewell to the child.

Mother Of Earth

On mornings such as these thoughts of you caress my mind,

swoon my heart to a tender beat.

I swear sometimes I am sure you are near me

I am certain that you can see and hear me

Mother of my earth sent from heaven by Mother of my birth.

A model of love, compassion, empathy and grace

No distinction between blood and water,

You showed me love and made me your daughter.

Mother of my earth sent from heaven by Mother of my birth.

In your words and ears of wisdom I did rely.

You've got moxy you always said to me

No limits, no boundaries to what I could be.

From the start this thing my art with father you did encourage.

...

Mother or my earth sent from heaven by Mother of my birth.

You raised me up like your own, never feeling like an orphaned child.

With your family you surrounded me, knowing in your heart

And in your mind that a child like me needs trees to climb.

I never told you this, for me it was simple fact

That from heaven Pearline sent you Arlene,

I know in my heart this is true.

You two must be spiritual sisters, from spirit to body electric.

No distinction between blood or water,

Time or space.

Such things made arbitrary by the powers of truth and grace.

Two mothers a blessing, a redemption, a love force and a guide,

An earth mother sent for a little girl child.

How lucky, how blessed to be touched by such a Mother of this earth

Sent from heaven

Heaven sent by the Mother of my birth.

Ritual

Ritual to bring water

Ritual to bring rain

Water to quench your parched earth

Water to quench your thirst.

We dance to bring down the baby

We dance the coming birth,

We stomp we drum down the dead

To carry the soul on ahead.

We sing and chant the pain away

We sing and chant insane away

They say to pray the devil away

And some to even make him stay.

On Your Sleeve

Do not wear your heart on your sleeve.

Let its blood flow ink words for your pen

Let its plasma hues pigment your brush

Let it color your canvas to deepest red.

Do not wear your heart on your sleeve

Let its chambers structure your sculpture.

Let its skin stretch tight to pound out a drum beat

Let its rhythm inspire your mantra to song

Let its muscle move your body in dance to flight.

Do not wear your heart on your sleeve.

Let its arteries to sustenance your rivers flow

Let its tears cascade from your highest peaks

Let its warm liquid rise to restore your torn flesh.

Do not wear your heart on your sleeve.

Let it bring forth new life to rest

Let it bring forth new life to rest

Let it bring forth new life to rest

To rest upon your beating breast.

A Solace For The Masochist

Fret not young scribe

All will be realized.

Once you have been accepted

You will eventually be rejected.

One Eyed Blind

Opiates come in many forms, they come in all kinds

They've got something in common, they all leave you one eyed blind.

Visual noise is designed to cloud and constrict the mind.

Your savior is of their design, it leads you to believe that a crime is not a crime.

Leaves you to believe that excess and greed is your only need.

Even conspiracy theories they define,

Have you saying, what do I need with my own mind.

Opiates come in many forms they come in all kinds

Sensory noise is created to fill the silent spaces where truth and inspiration reside.

Chain leashed to a magnetic one eyed pet upon which your life relies

Even redefine your sense of self, the selfie? Really?

Even old Narcissus in all his ignorance gazed into his own reflected eyes,

Gazed into his very own eyes as he was chilling down by the river side.

Dang ya'll are you really that resigned?

At least tell me you know and are willfully behind

At least tell me that you know you are one eyed blind,

That you know they are robbing your soul and mind.

...

Opiates come in many forms they come in all kinds

No need to blow it up your nose or shoot it in your vein,

Don't even need the hops or even the grain.

A pill ain't even needed to leave your senses subdued and depleted.

Chain leashed to your favorite one-eyed pet

That will suck up all your water to the desert dry

And tell you that you are soaking wet,

Your' all soaking wet, now you gotta know that's a lie.

But that opiates got you all on wind,

Its' truly got you one eyed blind.

As long as in that device you find it,

Never mind it.

Even got you telling yourself, I'm thirsty as hell

And I know I ain't really wet,

But please lawd please don't take away my one eyed pet.

Time And Space

Time and space it is relative they say

The smoke blowing from my lips is light years away.

It blew light years ago from a wood fire as the falling rain doused its rage

In the forest on the funeral pyre, leaving my ashes in its wake

Born tomorrow before I die yesterday.

Time and space is relative they say

It is the reason strangers I see - I know, but do not know me.

The trees felled tomorrow will tomorrow still grow,

They glow beneath feathered clouds in Bensonhurst or Long Island City

It is an Acacia tree and we are really in Nairobi.

It could be in Tarifah and the Levante is about to blow,

Or could it be in Mississippi, on Gibraltar, or in Morocco.

Time and space is relative they say

So here is really there. There is really yesterday and tomorrow was last year.

It happened on the sands of Galo Kinondo.

The camel that I did see, the camel it is now me.

The camel the conga and the moon's glow still to come

It came already tomorrow it vibrates it hums.

It is still to come yesterday, it hums it vibrates

Time and space is relative they say

It is all relative time and space.

What Does One Do

What does one do with a lover?

Does one give up the body easily?

Does one share mind, body and soul willingly

Or keep a bit back, save a little just for me.

What does one do with a lover?

Explore his landscapes like a hiker through the Rockies,

Climb his big strapping body like a mighty oak tree,

Should I let him manipulate me like silly putty?

What does one do with a lover?

Swim through his tears like a salmon up a stream,

Crawl on top of him in sleep and together with him dream.

Celebrate all of his and all of my vulnerabilities,

See his weakness for his strengths or overlook all of these

Profess we are only human and just leave it all to be.

...

What does one do with a lover?

Trade my-she for his-he, or is all of that arbitrary.

Should he cook and should I clean,

Should I let him be sweet while he lets me be mean?

What does one do with a lover?

Do we travel the globe over land and sea.

Should we trade ignorance for knowledge,

Holding our opinion at polar opposition

Or just agree and agree and agree.

What does one do with a lover?

Does one take the middle way,

Taking a grateful stance as we share each day?

What does one do with a lover?

When it all must go, when death interludes

And our hands must fall away.

What happens then, what does one do

When our time dear lover is completely through.

Smoke And Memory

I breath, I write, I paint, I live.

I have no questions I seek no answers

I have no truths to be proven or dispelled,

I hold no findings to be suppressed or upheld.

I breath, I write, I paint, I die.

No attempts at redemption to find

No hope no recrimination for human kind.

I am what I am to be, I am smoke and memory.

I propound no dogma

Am guided by no idiom manmade.

I am a moment in time that having been has become benign.

I breath, I write, I paint, I live, I am what I am to be.

I seek no justice no revenge, I observe with no opinion.

I speak no language, no native tongue, I hold no dominion.

I breath, I write, I paint, I live, I die, I am the truth I am the lie.

I am what others make of me, I am smoke and memory.

This

With a painters eye I observe life's multitudes

Written upon the land and the sea.

Life's full multitudes in all that I see.

Plant, animal, mineral, matter, humanity.

But beyond their exterior semblance it seems only one

Only one and the same face that gazes back at me.

How and what could this possibly be

That life could still hold for me this,

Such a sweet and singular mystery.

Life Is Mystery Love.

Parting Words

I come from a long line of mystic storytellers.

A peace loving creative born on Jamaican shores in the 60's, such a petulant time.

Blessed by life to a family, an ancestral lineage of inspired royal souls yet cursed by their constant leaving,

a paradox that keeps repeating and repeating.

Driven to journey the globe to touch its lands and seas, propelled to put color and word to textured memory.

Driven by passion and compassion, here is my greatest leap. I feel compelled to place the word and the image

side by side. They each seem to need their own space to speak, to live, to exist in their own stride.

Now in and out of prose I go to tell you the latest, what in my soul, mind and body resides.

And as the first poem goes, they tell me it is time.

Your journey through this books pages should be like a walk in the park, a nice walk that clears your head

and fills your heart. This volume is my first attempt at sharing sacred thoughts such as these,

if they touch you, if they move you then my ancestors and I shall be eternally pleased.

Pamella Allen

Index